SINGLE TO MARRIED IN UNDER A YEAR

A Christian Guide to Purposeful Dating with God's Leading

Rachel Gallagher

Single to Married in Under a Year: A Christian Guide to Purposeful Dating with God's Leading
© Copyright 2025 by Rachel Gallagher (nee Wenke)

No part of this publication may be reproduced or transmitted in any form or by any means, electronic or mechanical, including photocopy, recording, or any information storage or retrieval system, without permission in writing from the author.

ISBN: 978-0-9942734-7-5

All scripture unless otherwise stated is taken from World English Bible (public domain).
Scripture quotations taken from the Amplified® Bible (AMP), Copyright © 2015 by The Lockman Foundation. Used by permission. lockman.org

Contents

Introduction 7

Chapter 1: Getting the right foundation 11

Chapter 2: Keep asking, seeking, and knocking 19

Chapter 3: Identify your non-negotiables 33

Chapter 4: What could be holding you back? 41

Chapter 5: Be intentional 49

Chapter 6: Setting physical and emotional boundaries 61

Chapter 7: How to discern God's peace and leading 65

Chapter 8: Tactics from the enemy 75

Chapter 9: Waiting with purpose and joy 85

Invitation 91

Appendix 1: Internet dating tips 95

Appendix 2: Questions to ask before marriage 98

This book is dedicated to my incredible husband, Kim.
Every day, I am in awe of God's goodness
for bringing us together.

Introduction

Let marriage be held in honor among all...
Hebrews 13:4

Marriage is an incredible gift designed by God. It is the closest relationship that two human beings can have on earth, whereby two lives, that of a man and a woman, are merged as one. Within marriage, a husband and wife can become fully known yet fully loved - a beautiful reflection of the unconditional love God has for us and the relationship between Christ and the Church (Ephesians 5:25). Marriage is the opportunity to serve one another sacrificially for the well-being of the other and ultimately help fulfil God's will for one another's lives. Marriage also brings God great glory. My pastor once said, "Marriage is God's power plan to the earth, where two godly people move together as one".

For these reasons, our enemy and the god of this world (2 Corinthians 4:4), Satan, hates marriage. He uses countless tactics to prevent relationships between godly men and women from forming, or if they do begin, he will do all he can to stop them from progressing to marriage. This book was written to provide single Christians with purposeful advice on how to follow God's leading in their journey to marriage and to help expose and overcome, by the power of the Holy Spirit, strategies Satan may use against them.

Although now happily married, my journey to finding my husband spanned nearly twenty years. During this time, I learnt a number of insights and lessons I will share, which I pray will also be helpful to you. Unlike many Christians who marry in their twenties, I was in my late thirties and my husband in his early forties when we got married (as pictured). But good things come to those who wait! My husband, Kim, is my dream partner and was definitely worth the wait! The verse Ephesians 3:20 about God going  superabundantly above what I could hope, dream or imagine best describes how I feel about Kim. We can both honestly say that apart from knowing Jesus, our marriage has been the greatest blessing to our lives.

Now, you may be wondering from the book's title if it is realistic to go from single to married in a short time frame of under a year. Yes, it is not only possible - I also experienced it first-hand! My husband and I were engaged six months after meeting and married five months after that- going from single to married in under a year. We were both, however, very intentional in how we used our time to get to know each other, which gave us confidence in our decision to marry. As a result, we don't believe we rushed into marriage, but rather it happened in God's perfect timing. We are now enjoying a fruitful marriage and remain deeply in love and committed to one another. We are also honoured to be parents of a beautiful daughter.

Of course, God has a unique plan and timing for your life, and how your love story unfolds may look very different to ours. You don't need to feel rushed or pressured to get married in a certain timeframe, whether that is a year or something else - the main thing is you are led by God. I believe, however, that the strategies in this book will help you to be more intentional in your pursuit of marriage and avoid unnecessary delays and pitfalls - so that, like Kim and I, it's possible that you too may experience going from single to married in under a year.

Before we dive in, let me give a brief tour of the book to provide a bit of a roadmap of what to expect. The first couple of chapters explore some foundational and biblical principles needed in your journey to marriage, including strengthening your relationship and closeness with God and being proactive across three core areas of relationships. The book then gets more specific, unpacking topics including how to identify your non-negotiables in a partner, common reasons people delay their season of singleness or stay with the wrong person, and a focused guide on how to be intentional across each stage of dating. The last three chapters provide important insights rooted in Scripture into how to discern God's leading and identify and overcome tactics from the enemy related to pursuing marriage, and finally, how to wait with joy and purpose as a single. To make the book practical to your own situation, there are also reflection questions and action steps at the end of each chapter. I encourage you to take your time to reflect on these questions and have a spare notebook handy to write down your responses. That way, you can monitor your progress and make yourself accountable for the actions you commit to, getting the most out of what you've learnt.

While any single person can receive wisdom from this book, it was especially written for born-again Christians - those who are committed to live for Jesus as Lord of every facet of their life. If you've not yet made this commitment but are interested in finding out how, turn to page 91. One final thing before we begin - I invite you to take a moment to pray the following prayer from your heart. As you pray, know that my husband Kim and I are standing in agreement with you:

Dear Heavenly Father,
Thank you for knowing and caring for me more than I could ever comprehend. As I read this book, help me to surrender to Your Holy Spirit and receive the wisdom You want me to receive. Speak to my heart and lead me in Your ways and timing in the area of my relationships. May Your will be done in my life for Your glory.
In Jesus name,
Amen.

Chapter 1: Getting the right foundation

*But seek first the kingdom of God and His righteousness,
and all these things shall be added to you.
Matthew 6:33*

Regardless of whether you are single or married, for you to live the life God is calling you to and meet with Him in heaven, your relationship with God must always be your highest priority. Jesus said the greatest commandment is to *"love the Lord your God with all your heart, with all your soul, and with all your mind"* (Matthew 22:37). Everything else, including marriage, must pale in comparison to knowing and loving God. That's why even though marriage IS an amazing gift, it should never be the "be all end all" or ultimate goal or destination in your life. Marriage will not suddenly fix all your problems and should certainly never replace a dynamic and growing relationship with God through His Son, Jesus.

Similar to the greatest commandment to love God- the first commandment God gave to the Israelites was to have no other gods before Him (Exodus 20:3). You may think, "I'm fine, I don't worship any other gods"- but in God's eyes, another god or "idol" is anything we elevate or love more than Him. One way to expose an idol in your heart is to identify if there is any unwillingness to let go of something, even seemingly good things. For example, if you cannot surrender to God the idea of being married and be content with being single, marriage may be an idol. While marriage is a wonderful blessing, and there is nothing wrong with desiring it as a single, your desire for marriage should never compete with your desire for God.

Throughout my many years as a single, I had to continually check my heart to see that I wasn't elevating the desire for marriage above God. Whenever this unfulfilled desire started to steal my joy and cause me discouragement, the Holy Spirit would gently nudge me to come closer to Him. Through time connecting with God through prayer and worship, I would get to a place in my heart where I was completely content in God, regardless of whether I married or not. He alone was my joy. By continually surrendering my desire for marriage to God, I wasn't "giving up" on the idea of marriage - I still knew in my spirit I would get married and had a strong desire for it. I was simply putting this desire in its rightful place, beneath my greatest source of contentment- God, and believing that His will and leading for my life was the best path for me, no matter what that looked like.

To surrender to God and find contentment in Him above all else, you have to have closeness with Him. It's difficult to surrender to or trust someone you have a shallow relationship with. The truth is, there are no shortcuts to knowing God in an intimate or close way. Like a relationship with anyone is grown through shared experiences and time together, so is your relationship with God. You must draw near to God, and as His Word promises, He will draw near to you (James 4:8).

Drawing near to God is so much more than just going to a church service on a Sunday. It is a daily drawing of your heart and attention to be in communication with God- the Father, Jesus and Holy Spirit. Out of this relationship and your love for God comes a beautiful surrender of your need to be in control and be "master" of your life. You instead willingly surrender to Jesus being your Lord and Master so that He is directing and governing every area of your life. Yes, every area! That means not only your desire for marriage but what you watch on the internet, to what you buy, what you dwell on and who you spend time with. Being single is the best time to cultivate your relationship with God and develop this strong foundation of surrender and closeness with Him, which can continue to flourish once you are married.

Heart check
Right now, be honest with yourself, how would you describe your relationship with God? Is He your deepest source of joy in this life and your greatest love? Is He your highest priority above all else? It is not about your words, for God's Word says we can confess things with our mouth but our

heart can be far from Him (Matthew 15:8). Rather, how important God is in your life is reflected in your actions and how you spend your time - whether you are continually laying down your life in surrender and obedience to God in response to your love for Him.

All of us as Christians are called to continually grow from glory to glory (2 Corinthians 3:18) until we meet with Jesus, so we don't need to be perfect before we are married; we are all works in progress- married or single! However, here are a few questions which may illuminate how your relationship with God is currently travelling compared to other desires in your life, including marriage:

- Do you get more excited and passionate about the idea of getting married, social media, TV, video games, your appearance, health, politics, money, investments, shopping, or some other activity/interest than God and spending time in His Presence?
- Is your default mindset on things of God and heavenly things, or do you routinely think of worldly, carnal things and rarely think of God throughout your daily life?
- Do you regularly read your Bible and pray, or are these times few and far between?

- Are you growing and transforming slowly into the image of Jesus through obedience and surrender to Him, or do you continue to battle year in and year out in the same areas without any evidence of transformation?

If you were convicted by the Holy Spirit when reading any of these questions that perhaps you need to make some changes in your relationship with God - don't ignore this conviction. Embrace the invitation to come deeper in your relationship with God and ask Him to help you by the Holy Spirit to draw closer.

Benefits of closeness with God
Our motive for closeness with God and putting Him first should be simply the joy of loving and knowing Him. He is our great Reward! Even so, as a byproduct, there are some benefits you will experience from having a deeper relationship with God when it comes to searching for a partner.

- **You attract who you are:** You can't expect to meet a partner who is passionately pursuing Jesus, if you are not doing the same. Someone who is pursuing God with their whole heart wants the same in a partner. If they see your relationship with God is not a big priority they will likely not be as interested in seeing you as a life partner.

- **Being led by the Holy Spirit:** When your relationship with God is flourishing, you will find it easier to hear God's voice. Specifically, you will be able to discern more clearly from the Holy Spirit whether there are any red flags about a potential partner and also when God is giving you an open door or green light (we will cover this topic much more later). I definitely experienced this in my walk with God. During times when I was very distracted and not prioritising God, it took me much longer to discern His will. As a result, I unnecessarily prolonged relationships that were not the right fit compared to when I was walking more closely with Him.

- **Your happiness will not be from your partner:** No matter how wonderful your future partner is, they will never be able to meet all your needs; only God can do that. When God is your deepest love and greatest source of satisfaction, your cup will be full and overflowing. The happiness that comes from your partner will be an added blessing and bonus in your life, but not something you are dependent on to be happy. I have learnt this to be so in my own marriage. The "fuller" my cup is in God from fostering closeness with Him, the more joyful and at peace I am and the more of a blessing I can be to my husband and others.

In summary, throughout your journey in finding the right partner God has for you, make it your priority to always keep God your greatest love and to continually draw closer to Him.

Practical steps and reflection:
1. Do you desire marriage more than you desire God? If so, make more time to draw closer to God and ask Him to help you surrender so that you can find your contentment and joy in Him above all else.
2. Are there any distractions you need to eliminate from pursuing God with your whole heart?
3. Is there anything God has been asking you to do that you haven't done? Don't delay or put off obedience- walk in obedience now as an act of love and surrender to God.
4. What's one step or change you can make today to help strengthen your relationship with God?

Chapter 2: Keep asking, seeking, and knocking

Ask, and it will be given to you; seek, and you will find; knock, and it will be opened to you. For everyone who asks receives, and he who seeks finds, and to him who knocks it will be opened. Or what man is there among you who, if his son asks for bread, will give him a stone? Or if he asks for a fish, will he give him a serpent? If you then, being evil, know how to give good gifts to your children, how much more will your Father who is in heaven give good things to those who ask Him!
Matthew 7:7-11

Some people believe that they don't need to do anything and God will miraculously bring their partner to their doorstep. While nothing is impossible for God and He can most certainly drop a partner in your lap, we see in God's Word that this is more the exception than the rule. More often than not, God wants us to take proactive steps to receive His promises, all the while trusting in Him and His grace.

For example, if you were looking to buy a house, would you wait until God brought a person to your door offering to sell their house, or would you take intentional steps to find a suitable home - contacting a real estate agent, searching online, and inspecting homes? If you wanted a job, would you wait around until someone offered you one or actively apply for jobs and go to interviews? Why is it different to finding a marriage partner? God doesn't want you to passively wait for a partner, complaining that He's not moving when you are not taking any proactive steps yourself.

We see this principle at work in the Bible. Isaac sought out a wife, with his father sending his servants out to find Rebekah (Genesis 24). Ruth initiated a pursuit with Boaz at the threshing floor, boldly showing her interest in him (Ruth 3). In the same way, in Matthew 7:7, Jesus gives us a call to action, saying, *"Ask, and it will be given to you; seek, and you will find; knock, and it will be opened to you"*. Indeed, Kim and I applied this Scripture in our search for one another, which eventually led to our marriage.

This chapter will now describe how the principles found in Matthew 7 can be practically applied in your relationships to help in your journey to marriage. To start, let's break this verse down. In it, there are three action words: ask, seek, and knock. When it comes to relationships, the "asking" is relying on God's guidance, "seeking" is looking for a potential partner and "knocking" is initiating the next step. As shown in the diagram, these three actions are depicted as a cycle you journey through until you finally marry whom God has intended for you. Let's now look at each of these actions in more detail.

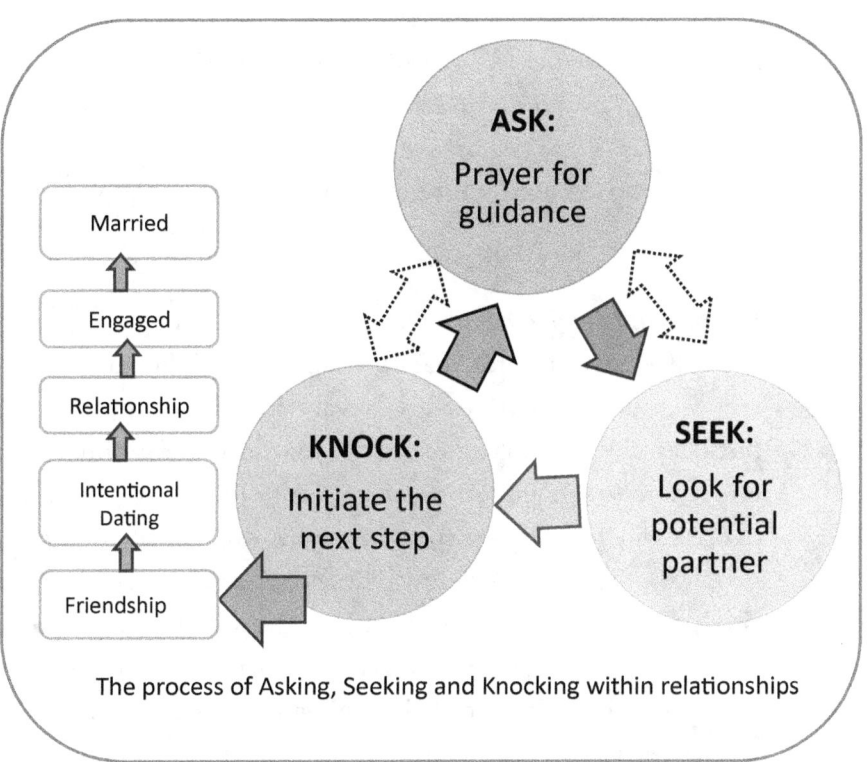

The process of Asking, Seeking and Knocking within relationships

1. Asking

Asking involves speaking to God through prayer to guide you to know His will for you. Everything we ask God is according to His will. As 1 John 5:14 says, *"And this is the boldness which we have toward him, that if we ask anything according to his will he hears us…"* Therefore, it is important to pray that God's perfect will is done. If you have a strong desire to be married, I personally believe God will provide a marriage partner for you if you cooperate with Him and follow His leading by the Holy Spirit. Like God provided for Adam a partner as we read in Genesis 2:18 (AMP) *"...It is not good (beneficial) for the man to be alone; I will make him a helper [one who balances him—a counterpart who is] suitable and complementary for him."* - God can provide a suitable partner for you.

If you don't have a desire for marriage

What if your desire for marriage isn't strong? Perhaps you feel pressure to marry or don't want to disappoint others, but deep down, you're not sure if marriage is for you. It's important to be honest with yourself. Jesus says certain people will remain unmarried *"for the Kingdom of Heaven's sake"* (Matthew 19:12). Some people have a gift of remaining single for the sake of serving God to advance His Kingdom. Jesus goes on to say, *"He who is able to accept this, let him accept it"* (AMP). If you are called to be single, then during the asking phase, when you are seeking God's guidance according to His will, you will get a sense that marriage is not the path God has for you (or at least not in this season). There will be grace and peace to accept this and live a rich and fulfilling life as a single person. Humble yourself and let go of your desires. As you seek in your heart God's guidance, He will make His will clear to you over time by His Spirit. Sometimes it is a gradual awareness, but you will know.

Also, be open to the fact that your desire for marriage might change. For example, for many years before we met, my husband, Kim, didn't have a desire to be married. This, however, changed a few months before meeting me when his heart's desire to have a family began to grow. God was calling him out of the season of being single into the season of marriage.

If you do have a desire for marriage
For those who do have a strong desire for marriage in this season, asking for God's help and guidance is essential. It is not just a one-off but something you continually do throughout the process of meeting someone (seeking) and before moving forward in a relationship (knocking). Apart from deciding to follow Jesus, marriage is the biggest decision you will ever make in your life, so it's important to have God's help throughout the process! Also, how can you expect to find and eventually marry a partner if you haven't asked God for His help? James 4:2 says, *"...you do not have because you do not ask."* For these reasons, I cannot emphasise enough the importance of asking God and leaning on Him throughout your journey to marriage.

Check your motives
Another important thing to consider when asking God for His guidance is being aware of your motives. As James goes on to say, *"you ask and do not receive, because you ask amiss, that you may spend it on your pleasures"* (James 4:3). We need to have the right motives for wanting to marry- to bring God glory and have a companion to share life with and love and

honour. Your motive shouldn't be to fill a void in your life that should be filled with God (see Chapter 1). When we ask God according to His will with the right motives, we can have confidence He has heard our prayer and that He will guide us in this area. 1 John 5:15 (AMP) further emphasises, *"And if we know [for a fact, as indeed we do] that He hears and listens to us in whatever we ask, we [also] know [with settled and absolute knowledge] that we have [granted to us] the requests which we have asked from Him."*

2. Seeking

The second action word highlighted in Matthew 7 is "seeking". Seeking means to "look for". Since you are confident that, according to God's will, He has heard your prayer during the "asking", you can now "look for" how He will bring His will to pass with confidence.

Be expectant

When seeking, you need to be expectant. So leave the attitude, "I'll never find anyone", "there's no good men out there", "all the good women are taken". These are lies from the enemy. Instead, replace these attitudes with, "I trust God will provide for me in this area", "In His perfect timing, I will meet a wonderful partner God has prepared for me". Jesus said, *"According to your faith be it done to you"* (Matthew 9:29). In other words, you will get what you believe. If deep down you don't really believe or expect you will get married, then you more than likely won't.

Even though I was actively looking for someone for many years before I met Kim, I always believed God had someone special reserved for me. While it was difficult at times and Satan did his best to discourage me, I didn't stop believing or having hope that it would all happen in God's timing – and that it did! If you are struggling with keeping hope while you are seeking, ask God to increase your faith and expectancy in this area while continuing to trust His plan for your life.

How do you seek?
In a practical sense, seeking means keeping a lookout for potential partners as you go about your daily life, as well as increasing your opportunities to meet different people, particularly Christian singles. This may be people at your church, social events, work, or any circles you move in, such as with your neighbours, friends of friends, people at the gym or even your bus route. If you have few opportunities to meet other people, especially other Christians who are single, you may need to be more intentional in your seeking. You might consider attending a Christian singles event or online dating. The latter was how Kim and I met, and many other Christian couples I know who are also happily married. Online dating can seem daunting for some, and I've included a section in Appendix 1 with some extra tips if this is something you want to consider. Being more intentional about "seeking" may also include joining a group

or class, volunteering to serve in the community or trying new hobbies with others. These activities may not only enrich your life but also widen your social circle to meet others.

Being intentional about "seeking" can take time and effort on your part. If you are a busy person but really want to get married, you need to make room in your week to meet others. When I was single, I was working full-time in a busy job and had a number of social and ministry commitments. Despite this, I knew in my heart that it was God's plan for me to marry, so I prioritised making time in my week to meet new people. While I was trusting God to provide, I wanted to cooperate on my end by being proactive and allowing opportunities to eventually cross paths with the man God had chosen for me.

For me, internet dating was a time-effective way of meeting other Christian singles who had marriage potential. However, it doesn't really matter how you find a potential partner. What matters most is whether, in the end, you have discerned that in God you are compatible. This is why, even when you find a potential person you may be interested in, you still need to ask God for guidance on how to proceed. (This is shown in the diagram, with the two-way arrow between "seeking" and "asking".)

If God gives you the green light to move forward with a potential partner, then you should progress towards the next step. That is where "knocking" comes in. This is where it starts to get exciting as you step out in faith!

3. Knocking

The knocking stage is the most action oriented of all the three stages. Let's use the analogy of knocking at a door. To do so, you need to know which door to go to, walk to the door and physically put your fist on the door, move your wrist and make a thud. You don't just ask where the door is and look for it which are the first two parts of Matthew 7:7 (ask and seek). You now need to interact with what is before you by taking the next step! In other words, you might have prayed to God to meet someone (the asking) and then looked and found a potential interest (the seeking) but nothing may happen unless you take a leap and ask that person out or at least show your interest in getting to know them (the knocking).

Knocking also is not a one off. It is needed before moving to each stage of a relationship. These stages are depicted on the left side of the diagram on page 21. They start from meeting a person and getting to know them as a friend, to intentional dating, formalising your relationship to boyfriend-girlfriend and then eventually engagement and marriage. Throughout these stages, you should continually ask for God's guidance before progressing to the next stage.

So again, the arrows between "knocking" and "asking" go in both directions.

In a practical sense, how do you knock? Let's use my and Kim's relationship as a working example. When I was single, I would continually ask God for His will in relationships that He would bring along the right partner in His timing (asking) and then while I was on the lookout (seeking), Kim contacts me through a dating website. From his profile picture I sensed an attraction and it stated he was a Christian but I didn't know much about him. The only way to find out if we were potentially compatible was getting to know him. This was where the knocking initially started. I had to take opportunities to ask Kim questions to find out about him and his relationship with God and see whether it was worth meeting in person. From taking this step (knocking), I sought God (asking) before proceeding to meeting him in person. Kim meanwhile was knocking by initially contacting me, and then also asking me questions to see whether he wanted to move forward in meeting with me in person. If we had met in a different setting, such as work or church, the same knocking would be required - proactively getting to know one another and showing interest to see whether or not to progress to the next step.

After meeting for the first time, Kim and I both continued to ask God for His guidance before progressing to the next stage in our relationship, including intentional dating, being boyfriend and girlfriend, engaged and eventually married. You may want to think of each of these different stages as a door that may be open or shut. We find out whether the door is open through prayer and a sense of peace to move forward (I will go through more about discerning God's peace in Chapter 7). With Kim, at every stage, I prayed, there was always an open door.

In contrast, a lack of peace may indicate a closed door or guidance to wait before moving forward. Sometimes, circumstances may also prevent you from moving forward. This may be the other person wanting to break up with you, having to move away or simply discovering you are not compatible.

Persistence
Before meeting Kim, every man I had started to get to know always led to a closed door. When I knocked on the door and asked God about moving forward to the next stage, there was always, at some point, a closed door. It's important to remember that even if you get a closed door or even like me - closed door after closed door after closed door - don't give up! It's important to be consistent and persistent. Don't think just because a relationship didn't work out that there is no hope for you. Keep asking, seeking and knocking. This is the intended meaning of the original language in this verse, as the Amplified version of Luke 11:9-13 describes:

"So I say to you, ask and keep on asking, and it will be given to you; seek and keep on seeking, and you will find; knock and keep on knocking, and the door will be opened to you. For everyone who keeps on asking [persistently], receives; and he who keeps on seeking [persistently], finds; and to him who keeps on knocking [persistently], the door will be opened.

If I'm completely honest, right before I met Kim, I was very tempted to give up on finding a partner. It was November, and that year I had been busy asking, seeking and knocking and gotten to know a number of Christian guys, one after another. All of them however, ended up being closed doors. I distinctly remember I was in my kitchen one evening, and I got clarity that the man I had been getting to know at a friendship level for several weeks was not the right fit, and to not progress anything further - another closed door! While my heart was not strongly attached to this man, I was tempted to be discouraged about yet another closed door. I remember crying out to the Holy Spirit, getting tired of the constant cycle of meeting someone and it not going anywhere. In that moment, I felt like the Holy Spirit was saying to my heart, "Don't give up, keep going, keep knocking!" I made the resolution I would keep going and trust God He would eventually bring the right man, and he would be well worth the wait.

I wasn't however expecting that God would answer this prayer so soon! Within a few minutes, I got an alert on my phone from a dating website that someone had sent a smiley face. I saw the notification and the man's profile photo and I instantly felt drawn to him. The next thought I remember having was, "I want to marry someone like him!" Well, it turns out that someone was not only very handsome but deeply loved God, met all my non-negotiables (more on this in the next chapter), and so much more. That man was Kim! I did end up marrying him, and to this day, he is still my dream man!

When Kim decided he wanted to find a partner to marry, he didn't have to do so much knocking. He met me only a few months after deciding to start seeking. For every person, the number of people you get to know as potential partners will vary, but if your journey seems to be prolonged, don't lose heart. Keep on asking, seeking and knocking.

Jesus said in Matthew 11:12, *"the Kingdom of Heaven suffers violence, and the violent take it by force."* To obtain all that God has for us as part of His Kingdom, we need perseverance, and sometimes we need to seize it with "force". That doesn't mean in a literal sense being violent or aggressive towards others to get married. It means having an inner resolve within you to keep going after what God has for you, despite any opposition you may be facing. The enemy will try to wear you down and discourage you so that you stop pursuing a marriage that is God's best plan for you. Don't give up, but rather wholeheartedly and in the power of the Holy Spirit, go after all God has for you!

This chapter has covered a lot of content; however, the takeaway is that meeting and marrying your dream partner takes action on your part. You can't be passive. Rather, you must cooperate with the Holy Spirit in persistent asking, seeking and knocking - trusting God's guidance and leading each step of the way.

Practical steps and reflection:
1. What action (asking, seeking or knocking) are you currently taking in your journey to marriage?
2. Are you asking God with expectant faith that He will guide you to His match for you? If not, ask God to increase your faith in this area.
3. If you are in the seeking phase, what can you do to widen your circles and opportunities to meet other Christian singles? Commit to one action this month - write it down and share it with a friend to be accountable.
4. If you have found someone you are interested in, are you actively "knocking" or taking steps to progress the relationship? If not, what could you do differently?

Chapter 3: Identify your non-negotiables

Don't be unequally yoked with unbelievers,
for what fellowship do righteousness and iniquity have?
Or what fellowship does light have with darkness?
2 Corinthians 6:14

When "seeking" a partner, if you want to use your time wisely and not prolong relationships with people who would not be compatible as a marriage partner, you must be very clear about what your non-negotiables are. The Bible has one clear non-negotiable for Christians- their partner must be a follower of Jesus. In addition to this non-negotiable, we will discuss in this chapter three other key areas of compatibility or non-negotiables.

Non-negotiable 1: They must be a believer
Paul writes that we are free to marry whoever we want as long as they are *"in the Lord"* (1 Corinthians 7:39), meaning they are a follower of Jesus or a born-again Christian. Therefore, it is unwise and goes against God's Word to pursue marriage with a non-Christian. It also clearly says in 2 Corinthians 6:14, *"Do not be unequally yoked together with unbelievers..."* This doesn't mean you can't be friends with non-Christians, but from my experience, it is unwise to begin a romantic relationship with an unbeliever, and the Bible is clear that you should not marry an unbeliever.

You might think, "Well, what if I can bring the unbeliever I'm interested in towards Jesus while we are dating?" While this can be true, you need to be very careful that you are being led by the Holy Spirit, as unfortunately, the enemy can bring unbelievers as romantic interests to draw the believer away from God. I know women who left their faith because they ended up dating and then marrying unbelievers. While this isn't always the case, it is risky. For example, unbelievers often do not understand or have the same physical boundaries as believers, which can lead to temptation to sin physically before marriage. Also, when you spend a lot of time with someone who is not governed by the Spirit of God and resisting sin by God's power, you may be exposed to sin in other areas, such as watching TV shows, movies or other media that grieve the Holy Spirit, swearing, gossip, carnal thinking or getting drunk. All of this can reduce your hunger for God and dull your conscience. Consider as well if you want to eventually raise a family together and encourage your children to follow Jesus. How will this work if your partner does not share the same beliefs as you?

If you are romantically interested in an unbeliever, keep some friendship boundaries up while you see how receptive they are to things of God. Do they show a genuine interest when you talk about spiritual things or quickly become disinterested and change the topic? Do they initiate questions or show curiosity about God, or are you always initiating these conversations? Are they interested in attending church with you? These things may help to gauge how ready the person is to receive the good news of Jesus.

Other areas of compatibility

Apart from a potential marriage partner being a Christian, what else is a non-negotiable? I remember having a long list of qualities that I wanted in a potential husband, but over time, my list of non-negotiables became much shorter and simpler. Things that I thought were important gradually became less so. My non-negotiables boiled down to needing compatibility in three broad areas:

-**Spiritual:** Are we in agreement about important spiritual matters? Does this person encourage my relationship with Jesus or hinder it?
-**Personality:** Do we have a growing emotional connection? Can I be myself around them?
-**Physical:** Am I attracted to them physically?

It was only from getting to know my husband, Kim, that I found compatibility in all three of these areas and knew that I had met the love of my life (second to Jesus!). With other men I dated, I always knew deep down something was missing. I never got this sense with Kim. Neither of us felt like we were settling or compromising in any way. In fact, I thought, "How blessed am I that I get to marry this amazing man!" Even years after being married, I still frequently think the same thing and praise God for bringing us together!

Let's now look a bit closer at these three key areas of compatibility to look for in a potential marriage partner:

Non-negotiable 2: Spiritual compatibility
Just because someone is a born-again Christian does not automatically mean you have spiritual compatibility or will agree on important spiritual matters. For example, one man I met strongly believed that the gifts of the Spirit were not for today and that we are once saved always saved, whereas I had opposite views. Despite deep discussions on these topics, we both knew that having these opposing beliefs would make a marriage together difficult. These may seem like minor things, but if we were to get married, it would be difficult to decide what we would teach our children on these matters and which church to attend.

An important sign of spiritual compatibility is that your partner encourages you to go after what God has called you to do and exercise the gifts He's given you. An even more important sign of spiritual compatibility is that the person and your relationship help draw you closer to Jesus - not away from Him. For example, Kim was extremely encouraging of my spiritual gifts right from the very start of meeting him. I could also see in his actions a consistent hunger for God and a desire to grow closer to Him and to help me in my walk with God.

Non-negotiable 3: Personality compatibility

Having a personality connection with someone can be described as being on the same "wavelength". There is an ease when you communicate with them. You both are comfortable in letting your guards down and feel completely relaxed in each other's presence. You also get an overall sense of feeling "safe" or at "home" in their company - that you will not be judged when you express your authentic self.

I knew Kim and I shared this compatibility when I could see my playful side coming out when I was around him. This part of me never came out in previous relationships, a side that only those in my inner circle ever get to see. When there is personality compatibility, you also stimulate each other's intellectual side and can have meaningful conversations on a range of topics. At the same time, you will feel completely at peace being in silence together, and you won't always feel the need to fill the silence with conversation. There is also no pressure to always be doing extravagant activities together. You simply enjoy being in each other's presence, no matter what you are doing.

Non-negotiable 4: Physical attraction

You can have compatibility at a spiritual and personality level, but unless there is a physical attraction, the relationship will just feel like a friendship. As you will read in the Bible's book of "Song of Solomon", the love between a husband and wife is meant to be passionate, a love known as 'eros'. You should feel attraction for one another and be physically drawn to that person. While physical attraction can grow, it is not something you can muster up. In previous relationships, I sometimes felt that I was being superficial because I didn't want to progress a relationship simply because I wasn't attracted to them. I came to realise, however, that God designed there to be an attraction between a man and a woman in marriage, and He would not want you to marry someone that you physically were not drawn to.

I can also see now how I prolonged certain relationships longer than they needed to be to try and "work out" if I was attracted to them physically. These men had many great qualities, and we were developing spiritual and emotional connections, but the thought of in the future kissing them or anything more after marriage didn't feel right at all. In contrast, when I first met my husband, there was never any doubt in my mind that I was attracted to him. While for some people attraction can grow, if after meeting someone a few times, you still have to ask yourself, "Am I attracted to this person?" you more than likely are not. It is likely best not to waste your or the other person's time pretending there is anything more than a friendship.

I wanted to highlight, however, that I intentionally put physical compatibility last out of the non-negotiables.

Although I believe physical attraction must be present, it shouldn't be the first thing you seek in a partner. If you ask someone what they love most about their husband or wife, very rarely do they say something physical- their hair or body shape. While you want to have physical attraction, looks fade and change over the seasons of life. That's why it's vital that personality and, particularly spiritual compatibility are present, as this is what your relationship will be grounded on for years to come. For example, both Kim and I said in our wedding vows that the thing we love most about one another is our love for God and our character.

Other non-negotiables
In addition to what you've read, you need to consider whether you have any personal non-negotiables. For example, Kim personally wanted to marry someone who hadn't been married before as he wanted to experience with his wife for the first time the wonder and newness of marriage and having a family together. For me, a non-negotiable was wanting to marry someone happy to live in the city I felt God was calling me to live in. Over the years, I was able to rule out a number of potential partners who lived in other states or countries who had no desire to live in the city I knew God had planted me in.

It's important to know very clearly what your non-negotiables are, as this will help refine and focus your search for God's best partner. It will also help rule out people you are not compatible with early on and potentially save you a lot of time in the process.

Practical steps and reflection:
1. What are your thoughts on only dating believers? Is this something you have done in the past? Will you make it a non-negotiable moving forward?
2. Reflect on whether you agree with the other non-negotiables- spiritual, personality and physical compatibility. Have you had this in previous relationships? Why/why not?
3. As you surrender to the Holy Spirit, write down what your non-negotiables are now. Refer back to this when you are getting to know someone to see whether it is a relationship worth pursuing.

Chapter 4: What could be holding you back?

*For God didn't give us a spirit of fear,
but of power, love, and self-control.
2 Timothy 1:7*

As you embark on your journey of asking, seeking and knocking, it is normal for things to take time. God's timing and ways are not the same as ours. While I thought I'd be married in my twenties, it took me until I was 38 to meet my husband- but God was right on time! If I had met Kim in my twenties, neither of us would have been ready for marriage. So the reason you're still single may be simply God's timing. However, if you've been putting God first as your greatest satisfaction in life, as described in Chapter 1, it may be wise to consider whether anything else may be holding you back or potentially delaying you from meeting your partner. Some common areas which we will discuss include procrastination, fear of the unknown, and unrealistic standards.

Procrastination

If you have had a desire to get married but haven't been on a date in several years, there may be some form of procrastination at work. This may not be the case if the Holy Spirit has led you for a season to first focus on other areas of your life or your relationship with God, in which case you must be obedient. However, if it seems like there is always some excuse or thing you are waiting to tick off before starting your search- it's more than likely procrastination. Maybe you're waiting on a promotion, to lose weight, or to get through another busy time at work. Whatever it is, you have to be honest with yourself - are these valid reasons to delay seeking a partner, or are they an excuse covering some deeper reason why you don't want to meet someone? Could it be that you're actually afraid of meeting the wrong person or deep down think you will never meet anyone? Do you feel like you are not enough? Is your heart still not healed from a previous relationship?

Ask God what the real reason is that you are hesitant to meet someone and to shine the light of His truth in this area. This may take some soul searching with Him, but once you have identified the deeper reason, replace it with His truth. For example, if you discover the underlying reason you're hesitant is thinking you are not good enough or no one will want to love you, meditate on the truth of God's Word in this area. That you are fearfully and wonderfully made (Psalm 139:14), that God loves you with an everlasting love (Jeremiah 31:3), and that you are the apple of His eye (Zechariah 2:8). Then once you believe this truth, take practical steps to start the process of meeting someone as described in the "seeking" section of Chapter 2, all the while leaning on the Holy Spirit's guidance.

Fear of the unknown

One reason why people procrastinate from dating can also be the fear of the unknown. As an introvert, I definitely had to step outside my comfort zone into the unknown to get to know potential partners. Initially, it was something I found very uncomfortable and nerve-wracking. I, however, felt God personally speak to me and encourage me that to enter the Promised Land in the area of finding a husband, I would need to conquer fear. For this reason, I decided not to let fear hold me back from meeting someone.

So if you are reading this and the idea of going on a date scares you, you are not alone! You may feel like staying in your comfort zone is protecting you, but it is actually doing the opposite. The longer you avoid meeting people because of fear (or procrastination), the harder and more daunting it becomes. On the flipside, from getting to know different Christian singles whilst keeping your boundaries, you can learn and refine your search and become more comfortable through the process. I'm personally grateful I didn't let fear rule me and prevent me from getting to know men through the friendship/dating phase. Through this process, I was able to define more clearly what I was and wasn't looking for in a man. When I met Kim, my now husband, it was much easier to discern that he was the right match for me.

So don't let fear or lies from the enemy hold you back from going after what God has for you. All of the greatest blessings in life are often obtained outside our comfort zone. As the saying goes, you've got to "risk it for the biscuit!" You often need to step into the unknown to receive the promises of God- that is the life of faith! When we step outside what is comfortable to us, we may feel out of control, but we can trust in the Comforter, the Holy Spirit (John 14:26). He is in control of the situation, and He has your best interest at heart. You can trust Him completely in the unknown because He is holding you. God's incredible love for you found in Jesus surrounds you and will give you strength. So shake off the fear, it's time to step out of the comfort of your boat and walk onto the water (Matthew 14:27-30)- knowing Jesus is right there with you!

Unrealistic standards
Another reason some singles may potentially delay opportunities from meeting the right partner is that they have unrealistic standards of what they are looking for. While we should not compromise on our non-negotiables, we also have to be realistic. My pastor once said, "Ladies, you are never going to find a man just like Jesus." It works the same for men- you are never going to meet the perfect "Proverbs 31" woman. We are all earthen vessels (2 Corinthians 4:7) with many flaws. None of us are perfect, but Jesus is, and as we look to Him, we can be transformed into His image.

The reality is, the closer we come to know someone, the more of their flaws we see. Similarly, as we gradually grow in being more authentic and comfortable with another person, the more our weaknesses will be seen. We shouldn't run away from relationships the moment we see something in our potential partner's personality that is short of perfection. Of course, there are definite red flags (I'm not talking about someone being verbally, physically or emotionally abusive). But if someone in a moment of weakness, uses a grumpy tone with you, or you have a disagreement and they say something that was not very kind, it doesn't mean you should instantly give up on them. Part of being in a relationship is learning to navigate through our imperfections and help one another to grow more like Christ. In fact, marriage was designed to be incredibly sanctifying in helping people be more like Jesus as they selflessly lay down their lives for each other.

When it comes to unrealistic standards, someone having a different background or upbringing from you does also not necessarily mean they should be ruled out. For example, when I met Kim, he had not been exposed to the same Pentecostal teaching that I had received over the past decade, and he wasn't baptised in the Holy Spirit or walking in any spiritual gifts. (For those not familiar with baptism of the Holy Spirit, this is something I encourage you to read further in Acts 1:5 and Matthew 3:11). Anyway, because of this, my natural self was a bit wary and thought this relationship probably won't work as walking in the fullness of the Holy Spirit was foundational in my walk with God and how I wanted to raise a family. I prayed to God about this and felt the Holy Spirit lead me not to try to change Kim's views or teach him, but to let God teach him in this area. I knew if I saw a change in Kim, it wasn't because of anything I had done- it was all God. Well, God exceeded all my expectations and I witnessed Kim become increasingly hungry for things of the Holy Spirit and eventually become gloriously baptised in the Holy Spirit. I've witnessed him demonstrating supernatural manifestations of the Holy Spirit's activity and shared with him glorious times in God's presence. My point here is that while we should not compromise on our non-negotiables, we also have to be open to God moving. We need to be led by God in all things and not rule people out just because they may be different to us.

Practical steps and reflection:
1. Do you always have a reason for putting off meeting someone? If this applies to you, ask God to reveal by the Holy Spirit if these things are masking a deeper reason that doesn't line up with His Word, and then replace that with God's truth.
2. Write down an action step you can do now to start your search (e.g., joining a singles group or an internet dating site, volunteering in a new capacity somewhere in your church or community). Put it in

your calendar and tell a trusted friend to keep you accountable to doing this action within the next 4 weeks.
3. Do you have an underlying fear of the unknown holding you back? Meditate on the truth that God is always with you, surrounding you with His perfect love that casts out all fear (1 John 4:18). Ask yourself, if God is with me, why should I fear?
4. Remember your non-negotiables. Are there any standards you have that you may need to let go of that are not part of your non-negotiables?

Chapter 5: Be intentional

*A man's mind plans his way [as he journeys through life],
But the Lord directs his steps and establishes them.
Proverbs 16:9 (AMP)*

Now that you have identified what might be holding you back, it's time to move forward with purpose. Dating or being in a relationship with a potential partner can be a wonderful time, enjoying one another's company and sharing experiences together. Its primary purpose, however, isn't to simply have fun or have a new companion of the opposite sex. The ultimate purpose of dating is to get to know as much of a person's true personality and character until you can clearly decide with God's guidance whether or not this is the person you should marry.

Being intentional allows you to reach this decision much sooner. If you are not intentional, 6 months, 12 months, or even 2 years can go by in a relationship, and you are not any closer to getting clarity about whether you should marry. If a relationship doesn't work out and you realise someone isn't God's match for you, you haven't failed. You've achieved the purpose of why you started dating in the first place- to decide whether you should marry or not!

Being intentional is a balance between being present in each other's company, whilst being purposeful in getting to know each other to determine their suitability as a potential marriage partner. You have to be careful, however, you don't become so fixated on whether or not they are "the one", that you put unnecessary pressure on the relationship or go down a rabbit warren of overthinking (more on overthinking later!).

So how do you stay intentional but remain in the moment? My biggest advice is not to jump too far ahead and take one step at a time.

Take one step at a time
God lights the path before us (Psalm 119:105), but often it is only the next step to take. Therefore, when you initially meet someone, your prayers don't need to jump ahead to, "Will I marry this person?" "Is he/she the one?" but rather "Is this someone I should invest time in getting to know?" Your prayers, however, will change the closer you move towards marriage. I've found from experience that there are usually five key stages from meeting to marriage that you will progress through as follows:

1. **Friendship/acquaintance:**
2. **Intentional dating**
3. **Relationship**
4. **Engagement**
5. **Marriage**

Of course, there is no set formula and each relationship is unique. This is just a guide that may reflect most people's journey, including how Kim and my relationship unfolded. Although rare, some couples might, for example, progress straight from a friendship to engagement.

The man in the relationship also generally initiates when to move to the next stage, particularly as things get more serious. This aligns with God's Word where Paul talks about the husband leading the wife in marriage (Ephesians 5:23) – so it's good practice for the man to show leadership in the relationship. Even so, for the ladies, that doesn't mean that you can't initiate getting to know someone more in the early stages and can just be passive and wait for the man to do everything. The main thing is that you are both led by the Holy Spirit and move in step with Him.

In the next section, we will now walk through each of these stages leading up to marriage, including what prayer points you may want to consider and what should be your main focus during each of the stages.

1. *Friendship/acquaintance- don't assume ask*
This is the first stage where you have met someone but the relationship is purely platonic. You may be having conversations with one another in a group setting, as friends one-on-one, or through email or text (if you met online),

but neither of you have directly expressed interest in the other in a romantic sense.

It's good to be aware during this stage that there are a lot of "nominal" Christians out there - those who confess to be a Christian by name but who do not have a personal relationship with Jesus or place any importance on following Him. To probe where someone is in their walk with God, you can ask questions in conversation like "What does being a Christian mean to you?" or "How important is your Christian faith in your life?" This was one way, for example, I could "screen" potential prospects when meeting people online to see whether it was worth catching up in person.

Prayer point:
Reveal to me by the Holy Spirit if I should invest time in getting to know this person more.

Focus:
The focus of this phase is finding out through your interactions:
- Do they have a genuine relationship with Jesus?
- Do you enjoy conversations with them?
- Are you attracted, or could you see yourself potentially being attracted to them?

If all answers are yes and there are no red flags in God then you should move to the next stage and ask them on a date or make it clear to them you are interested in getting to know them more. This might be as simple as saying, "I've enjoyed our conversations and would be great to get to know you some more to see if there could be anything between us. Do you want to go out for a coffee this weekend?"

2. Intentional dating- getting to know each other

During the dating phase, you are being intentional about spending more time with this person to get to know them. While you have indicated an interest in getting to know each other more to see if there is potential for a relationship, you are still keeping boundaries and things don't necessarily need to be overly romantic. Activities that allow for lots of conversation are ideal and can include anything you enjoy doing - whether it's rock climbing, nature walks, having a meal together, going out for coffee, or group activities. It doesn't have to be fancy or expensive and there shouldn't be lots of pressure.

Prayer point:
Guard my heart while I get to know this person more to see how compatible we are.

Focus:
The focus of this phase is finding out through conversation:
- Is this someone who has growing compatibility spiritually, personality/emotionally and I'm physically attracted to? (see Chapter 3)
- Can I be myself around them?
- Do they meet my non-negotiables as a potential marriage partner?

If the answers are yes and you have an open door in God, consider discussing progressing to the next stage into a more formal relationship.

3. Relationship – Getting to know them and their world more deeply

In a relationship, it is established that you are now officially a couple or "boyfriend" "girlfriend" as many would say. Although things are getting more serious you don't need to feel rush or pressured. The focus now should be about spending more time enjoying each other's company in a variety of situations and settings. You want to get to know each other's worlds as much as you can. This includes being intentional about having different experiences together in everyday life - not just romantic dinners or movies. You also want to observe the other person when things may not be going to plan. When they are squeezed or under pressure what fruit or character traits come out?

It's also important to get to know those important to them- their family and friends and have them meet yours. It so happened through circumstances that Kim met my parents and sister very early on after we met. It was encouraging to see that my family all got a very good impression of Kim, and similarly, when I met his family, they had an equally positive impression. Our friends and family can sometimes see blind spots or things we fail to notice. If a number of your close friends and family do not get a good impression or do not think you are well-suited to your partner, this is a red flag and definitely something you should seek God about further.

Ask intentional questions
Throughout our relationship stage, particularly before we got engaged, Kim and I were very intentional in asking each other lots of questions to find out as much as we could about one another. This included going through a list of questions in the Christian book "101 Questions to Ask Before Getting Engaged" by Norman Wright. Some of the questions seemed quite confronting, but it's much better to bring to the light any potential areas of incompatibility early on to see if you can work through them before getting married. Many couples fail to discuss basic compatibility over things like how many children they want, where they would live and their views on marital roles. Once you are married, it's too late- it is for life! In Appendix 2 (page 98)

are over 60 example questions to consider asking before you get married. Of course, you can access other books and resources for a more exhaustive list.

Prayer point:
Help me see their true character, our compatibility and anything that may help decide whether we should move forward towards marriage.

Focus:
-Is this someone with whom I am compatible on a spiritual and personality level and physically attracted to?
-Is this someone I want to spend the rest of my life with?
-Do we sense God's peace and pleasure in moving forward and have the blessing of those close to us to progress to marriage?

If the answer is yes to all these questions, you should both seriously consider getting engaged.

Engaged- Preparing for marriage
The final stage before marriage is being engaged. For me, this was an exciting time knowing I would soon be married to the man of my dreams! It's also important not to get caught up in all the busyness of planning a wedding that you are not prepared for the marriage itself. Remember, the wedding is one day, your marriage is for the rest of your life.

You want to be intentional about discussing in a practical sense how your lives will merge after marriage, including where you will live, how your finances will be organised, how you will share the housework and so forth. Once engaged, Kim's pastor recommended we read a workbook together to prepare for marriage. Some couples may do pre-marriage counselling. While this is not essential, it is wise to do some kind of intentional preparation to ensure you have asked the important questions of each other, rather than going in blindly. Knowing Kim and I were on the same page about our core values and lifestyle choices, including important things like our preferences for having children and where we would go to church, made me more confident as well in my decision to marry Kim.

Prayer points:
- Guide us on how to best prepare for marriage.
- Expose anything in the other person that I've failed to see before we get married that you want me to see.

Focus:
- How will we merge our lives after marriage? Consider pre-marriage counselling to prepare for marriage.
- Is there anything coming to light that would give me reason not to marry this person?

- Do I still want to marry this person and sense God's peace in our decision to marry?

Engagement can truly be such an exciting time as you prepare to make a holy covenant before God to be husband and wife. Remember however, if anything does come up during this stage that makes you strongly question whether you still want to marry this person, then you should not proceed forward and either delay getting married or end the relationship. It is much better to listen to the leading of the Holy Spirit (see more in Chapter 7 about this) and be true to this than enter a marriage that is not God's best for you. It may feel embarrassing or cause inconvenience now, particularly if you have made wedding plans, but this is nothing compared to the magnitude of a lifelong commitment to someone you are not compatible with.

When there's a closed door
One last point, regardless of whether it's during the engagement or after a few dates, when you get the revelation that someone is not God's best for you and know with clarity that you do not want to marry them, then the wisest thing you can do is to end the relationship as promptly as possible. Of course, you must use discretion and plan the best time to have the conversation, particularly if it is a longer-term relationship, but don't put it off or procrastinate. The sooner you make the break, the sooner

you can both move forward and continue the search for the person with whom you do have compatibility.

Practical steps and reflection:
1. How diligent have you been in getting to know someone you were interested in, whilst dating or in a relationship?
2. Have you ever made a wrong assumption about someone because you didn't explicitly ask them about something in the earlier stages?
3. What's one thing you would do differently to be more intentional in getting to know someone throughout the stages of a relationship?

Chapter 6: Setting physical and emotional boundaries

*Keep your heart with all diligence,
For out of it is the wellspring of life.*
Proverbs 4:23

You often hear in Christian circles a lot about being careful with physical boundaries in dating, but not so much about emotional boundaries. It's important to be mindful of both when you are embarking on any potential romantic relationship.

Physical boundaries
The Bible is very clear that we as believers should be free from sexual immorality, which includes any kind of sexual activity outside the marriage covenant. The Bible is clear that sexual immorality is a sin which hurts us and God and has eternal consequences for your salvation (1 Corinthians 6:9-10). It's important to understand that we keep ourselves pure from any form of sexual immorality. The Amplified Bible says this in 1 Corinthians 6:18-20:

"Run away from sexual immorality [in any form, whether thought or behavior, whether visual or written]. Every other sin that a man commit is outside the body, but the one who is sexually immoral sins against his own body. Do you not know that your body is a temple of the Holy Spirit who is within you, whom you have [received as a gift]

from God, and that you are not your own [property]? You were bought with a price [you were actually purchased with the precious blood of Jesus and made His own]. So then, honor and glorify God with your body."

Unfortunately, there are many men and women who claim to be "Christians" who do not practice what the Bible states here. That's why, just because someone is a Christian, you can't assume they have the same boundaries as you. The specific physical boundaries you decide to practice are a personal thing and something you need to seek God about. As a general rule, however, you should avoid anything that tempts you to be sexually immoral or lust after the other person, which may differ between people. Things like sleeping in the same bed, heavy kissing and touching are playing with fire, even if you think you are not "doing the deed". If it is causing you to think lustful thoughts about the other person, then it is a sin.

Take things slow
While it may be very normal in the world to kiss someone on the first date, believers should take things slowly when it comes to physical affection and tread very carefully. Getting too physical too quickly, even with seemingly innocent things like hand holding and kissing, can create a rush of emotions and a euphoric and giddy-like state, which can impair your judgment. When you hold someone's hand, cuddle or kiss, your body receives a flood of "happy

hormones" including dopamine and oxytocin that your body starts to crave increasingly more. Some researchers even describe these early stages of romantic love as being comparable to drug addiction![1] Therefore, be very mindful of not rushing into being physically affectionate - that way you can see clearly who the other person is and not just through rose coloured glasses. You have your whole marriage to explore your physical connection. Focus on getting to know the person outside of the physical first- their spiritual walk, their character and personality. You will then be honouring God by keeping your relationship pure and having a clear conscience before Him.

Emotional boundaries
Physical affection aside, in the initial phases of meeting someone you find attractive, it's also very easy for feelings to take flight, and before you know it, this person is the only thing you are thinking about! You are already starting to picture what it would be like being married to them and how many children you would have, and you have barely started getting to know them. These feelings of infatuation can be confused for love and can also make it difficult to discern and see a person clearly for who they are. For these reasons, it's wise to be intentional about also setting some emotional boundaries for yourself.

---

[1] Zou Z, Song H, Zhang Y, Zhang X. Romantic Love vs. Drug Addiction May Inspire a New Treatment for Addiction. Front Psychol. 2016 Sep 22;7:1436. doi: 10.3389/fpsyg.2016.01436.

Until you are clear the person has very high potential as someone to marry, you need to be very careful to guard your heart (Proverbs 4:23). In a practical sense, this means not opening your heart too quickly to someone by revealing your innermost secrets, fantasising about your future and rushing into expressing things which can create premature emotional intimacy such as saying, "I love you". I made this mistake in earlier relationships only to discover as I got to know them more, that we weren't compatible. I then had the difficulty of needing to end a relationship with someone whom I had formed a strong emotional attachment to and felt "in love with". As a result, I ended up feeling broken-hearted and in need of healing. I learnt from this process to only open my heart when I had the green light from God to do so, and where there was significant compatibility (which was with Kim- my now husband!).

Practical steps and reflections:
1. Have you set physical boundaries before in previous relationships? After reflecting on God's Word about sexual immorality, what boundaries would you set in your next relationship to honour God? Be specific.
2. Moving forward, what's one practical thing you want to do to guard your heart emotionally in relationships as you journey towards marriage?

Chapter 7: How to discern God's peace and leading

Let the peace of Christ [the inner calm of one who walks daily with Him] be the controlling factor in your hearts [deciding and settling questions that arise].
Colossians 3:15 (AMP)

As touched on in Chapter 2, asking for God's guidance throughout your journey from singlehood to marriage is crucial. But in a practical sense, how do you discern His leading and guidance? How do you know God is giving you the green light to move forward? I don't claim to have all the answers when it comes to hearing from God, after all, we all only see in part or "dimly" (1 Corinthians 13:12). I will share, however, some practical things I've learnt through the Word and in my journey to marriage that may help you.

The first steps to seeking God's leading are to simply ask God to lead you and then trust that He will answer. This might seem obvious, but it is surprising how many Christians don't do this when it comes to dating. Asking God for His help and trusting Him takes humility. Rather than the attitude, "I've got this", it should be "God, you've got this, and I know You will lead me." God's Word promises us that those who are His children (if you've been born-again, then that is you!) know His voice and He leads them. In fact, God wants to lead you more than you want to be led by Him. It's the Holy Spirit's role to be our Guide! He wants to partner with you in all areas of your life- including your relationships. It's important we not only ask for God's guidance but also expect wholeheartedly that we will receive it. As Jesus says, *"Therefore I tell you, all things whatever you pray and ask for, believe that you have received them, and you shall have them."* (Mark 11:24).

So we can have absolute confidence that if we ask God to lead us, He will. It's simply our job to follow Him. How God leads you is up to Him and He can choose to lead you through different ways. The Bible talks about God leading His children through a still small voice (1 Kings 19:12), visions, dreams (Acts 2:17), and from other believers (Proverbs 11:14). God also commonly leads us through His peace (Colossians 3:15).

What is God's peace?
Romans 8:6 says, *"For the mind of the flesh is death, but the mind of the Spirit is life and peace".* When we are in the Spirit, our mind is surrendered to the Holy Spirit and thinking thoughts He approves of and in alignment with God's will. In this state of surrender, we will experience a sense of life and peace.

Peace is an inner knowing that all is well. While being at peace can give you feelings of calmness and being relaxed, we have to be careful not to base decisions on "feelings" of peace, otherwise we can be swayed in different directions by our fluctuating emotions. This may include our own desires creating a false sense of "peace", as Proverbs 14:12 says, *"There is a way which seems right to a man, but in the end it leads to death."* Just because something "feels right" doesn't mean it is. Emotions in our flesh can also take away our "feeling of peace". For example, the enemy may amplify feelings of fear and doubt which can be interpreted as God not approving of a situation when it is just our emotions.

The reality is that God's peace is deeper than a feeling; it is a "knowing" within. The Bible talks about God's peace surpassing all understanding (Philippians 4:7). So to surpass our understanding, peace must go beyond our soul, where we have our mind, will and emotions, to the deeper place of our spirit. Peace is a sense deep within that you know that you know something and that your thoughts, words and actions are in alignment with the Spirit, even if in the natural things may seem chaotic.

In the context of my relationship with Kim, after getting engaged, we set a date to marry about four and a half months away. For many, particularly the bride-to-be, wedding planning can be stressful, especially if you are doing it in a short time. However, this was not my or Kim's experience. We both had a deep knowing within all was well, there was an alignment and a deep peace amidst all the busyness of planning.

An absence of God's peace

On the contrary, when there is the absence of God's peace, there is confusion within. You experience restlessness and a nagging sense that something isn't right. This is common during times of high pressure, but sometimes an absence of peace can come even though your circumstances may seem like everything is going well. For example, during the "asking" phase of seeing whether you should move to the next stage with a person (whether that be from dating to relationship or relationship to engagement), you might sense something niggling or protesting deep within you. You might try to ignore this sense of unease or drown it out with justifications in your thinking, like "That's just the devil", "This person is a good match for me". You may even pray to God for this agitation within to go, but it is always there in the background. Something is not in alignment with God's will.

I have experienced this lack of peace in all my relationships that did not lead to marriage. Something didn't seem right. Even if the man I was dating had many great qualities and was a man after God's own heart, when it came to progressing the relationship forward, particularly the thought of marriage, a restlessness and uneasiness followed.

This lack of peace indeed was the Holy Spirit prompting me that marriage with any of those gentlemen was not His best plan for me. Over time, God revealed the reason for this unpeace which related to different areas of incompatibility. I could have married these men, but God knew that it would be much more difficult for us in the marriage than if I waited for the man where I did sense His peace- and I'm so glad I did!

Whenever you sense this lack of peace within, it is an invitation to seek God more wholeheartedly regarding what you are experiencing. Galatians 5:22-23 says, *"But the fruit of the Spirit is love, joy, peace, patience, kindness, goodness, faithfulness, gentleness, self-control…"* When we yield to the Holy Spirit, we experience His peace. A sign of not experiencing His peace can therefore be that there is an area of your life that you are not surrendering to God. It may be the Holy Spirit trying to communicate to your spirit that the relationship you are in is not God's best for you. God knows both of you, the future and how your pairing would result in terms of compatibility and effectiveness for His Kingdom.

So having God's peace, that inner "knowing", is important in discerning God's leading. This next section will explore other general tips to discern God's guidance, as well as things to be aware of to resist.

If you're not sure, don't move forward.
As detailed in Chapter 2, it's important to seek God's guidance throughout the relationship stages. An open door is a sense of ease and "knowing" in your spirit to move forward. A closed door is a clear "no" in your spirit. Sometimes, however, it's not always clear whether or not to move forward. Derek Prince, in his book "God is a Matchmaker", made an important point that when it comes to marriage, an "I'm not sure" should be treated as a "no" or at least a "not now"[2]. Don't move forward until you have clarity to do so.

God leads us by still waters (Psalm 23:2)
Sometimes we don't get clarity on what to do in a situation because we are too noisy in ourselves. Inside, we have such strong emotions. God can't speak to us when our own will or desires are louder than His. To discern how God is leading us, we need to get to a place of stillness or "rest" within. This means laying everything down at the feet of Jesus and having a heart's posture that says, "I want Your will, Father, not my own, whether that is one way or the other, to stay with this person or not, I am okay with the outcome". When you have this heart's posture, discerning God's leading is much easier. Sometimes God is trying to tell us something, but our desires are so strong we don't

---

[2] Derek Prince and Ruth Prince (2011). God is a Matchmaker: Seven Biblical Principles for finding your mate. Chosen books, Baker Publishing, USA.

want to hear it. And when we do hear it, we try to ignore it or deny it was God because it doesn't line up with what we want.

Relax!

Trying to discern God's leading is easier when we are completely relaxed. Sometimes, if we are trying too hard and putting too much pressure on ourselves to hear from God, we can get all worked up and frazzled. In this state, it is very difficult to discern anything. That's why, rather than straining and striving to hear God's direction, present your requests to God and just leave it with Him. That means not thinking constantly, "Is he or she the one for me? Am I doing God's will?" Sometimes the best thing you can do is not think about that, and just do something to relax, whether it's going to the beach, for a walk or doing some other pastime you enjoy. Whilst you are enjoying life, trust that God will speak to you rather than straining to hear from Him.

Overthinking leads to worry

We have to be very careful that we are not over-reasoning and rationalising things in our thinking. This in itself can cause you to lose the sense of God's peace. While it is important to think things through and use wise judgment and intentionality as described in Chapter 5, there comes a point when reasoning in your mind becomes overthinking, which can quickly lead to worry. Worry can be described as the absence of peace, often being an unease or anxiety about a problem or the future. Worry is a sin as Jesus commands against it (Matthew 6:34). We can't worry and experience God's peace at the same time. Sometimes a believer may think they are experiencing God's unpeace and will stop moving forward in a relationship when it is actually fear and worry. Therefore, it's important to relax, and repent of and reject any worrying or fearful thoughts.

Over-spiritualising
Another thing which can hinder discerning God's guidance is over-spiritualising. While we want to be spiritually minded, "over-spiritualising" can occur when we read too much into things in a spiritual sense which can lead us astray. While God can speak through circumstances and situations, these should confirm what you already know. They shouldn't be used as evidence to rationalise in your mind why you should stay with someone despite knowing deep down that something is not right. An example of this for me was several years ago, when I kept dating a man despite a lack of peace on the relationship because whenever I prayed with him, I would sense the tangible presence of God. I read into this thinking that this sense of God's presence while we prayed was God showing His approval of the entire relationship. The thing was I sense God's tangible presence when I pray with my friends or my sister - this doesn't mean that I am meant to marry them! After I broke up with this man, God highlighted this distinction to

me and corrected me on my misinterpretation of the situation. Similarly, just because you had a serendipitous way of meeting a person, that their street number is the date of your birthday, or their name means something of significance to you, does not mean you should take this as a spiritual "sign" of God's approval. If we are not careful, we can use these "signs" to try and fit with the outcome we want rather than surrendering to God's leading.

Seek wise counsel
Sometimes, other people in your life can see blind spots and help confirm God's leading. Proverbs 11:14 (AMP) says, *"Where there is no [wise, intelligent] guidance, the people fall [and go off course like a ship without a helm], But in the abundance of [wise and godly] counselors there is victory."* For example, when dating one gentleman many years before I met Kim, I was experiencing a lack of God's peace but felt conflicted as I had strong feelings for this person. I remember crying out to God one morning and asking Him to speak through others to help me discern what to do. Surely enough, the next day at church, three independent people spoke to me, confirming this person was not God's best for me without me even bringing it up. This timely counsel gave me the courage I needed to end this relationship.

In summary, it is God's role to lead and guide us by the Holy Spirit, and often He does this through a deep knowing or peace in our spirit. As we relax and put our trust in God, we can have confidence that He will lead us and confirm His will for us.

Practical steps and reflections:
1. Can you think of a decision you made or a situation where you sensed God's peace and one where His peace was absent?
2. Has the peace of God guided you in previous relationships? If yes, did you follow God's guidance or ignore it?
3. Is there anything that may be hindering you from experiencing God's peace to guide you? For example, overthinking or not dying to your own desires. What could you do differently that may help to discern God's leading by the Holy Spirit?

Chapter 8: Tactics from the enemy

The thief only comes to steal, kill, and destroy. I came that they may have life and may have it abundantly.
John 10:10

Satan hates marriage and will do everything he can to stop two godly people from meeting and, more importantly, marrying. It's his job to steal, kill and destroy believers. So even if you do meet the right person, you can expect some level of opposition. As the Israelites found giants in the Promised Land, when you are taking new territory in God, there is more likely than not going to be some kind of opposition from the enemy. But we do not need to fear, we have the victory in Jesus as He has overcome all the powers of the enemy (Colossians 2:15).

Kim and I experienced our share of opposition on our journey to marriage, but praise God, we persevered through it and overcame these battles and are now enjoying the fruits of a beautiful marriage. To offer some practical guidance in this area, the following chapter will highlight some general strategies Satan may use to hinder you from meeting or moving forward with God's best for you.

Attack on your thinking
One way to know if the enemy is at work when it comes to your thoughts can be an unrelenting driving pressure on the

mind to think certain thoughts. I had first-hand experience of this attack from Satan in my relationship with Kim in the area of fear and worry. We were both sensing that God was leading us to move things forward, and we were beginning to have serious conversations regarding progressing towards marriage. During this time, I remember some instances when I would get bombarded with thoughts to break up with Kim, accompanied by other fearful thoughts, "Oh no, am I doing the right thing? What if God is not in this and I'm missing God's will?" These thoughts were very pushy and not based on anything Kim had done, and also brought confusion. I remember one afternoon after battling with these thoughts all day at work, trying to keep it together, I got in the car and felt the Holy Spirit rise up in me, prompting me to command the demon harassing me to leave in Jesus' name. I did this and instantly felt the dark cloud of fear hovering over me disappear and my peace return!

When you are experiencing pressure on your thinking about certain negative thoughts - resist the devil, casting him out in the name of Jesus and he will flee (James 4:7). Remember, the authority you have over all the power of the enemy in Jesus (Matthew 28:18). Once you have cast out the devil, don't make any more agreement with any fearful or worrying thoughts from Satan. Instead, keep your mind renewed by the truth of God's Word unto you (Romans 12:2).

Devil masquerading as God
Sometimes the devil can also confuse believers by speaking to them, masquerading as an "angel of light" or the voice of God (2 Corinthians 11:14). You may hear a voice telling you "He is going to be your husband" or "She is going to be your wife" to confuse you when it is not God at all saying this but actually the enemy. Sometimes these thoughts can also be from our natural self and desires. You may even get dreams or visions with an impression that you are meant to marry someone when it is not God's best plan for you.

Dreams, visions and signs
While God does give dreams, we have to be very careful in interpreting dreams and using them as the final source of truth. Dreams and visions should confirm what we already know in our spirit and not be a fresh revelation to guide us. I have had dreams of marrying various people who were not my husband. These dreams may have been the enemy or may have been my own soulish nature, but I've learnt to take them lightly and weigh them up according to the peace of God, that knowing within, as described in the previous chapter, as well as God's Word.

Kim and I have also had dreams from the enemy trying to sabotage our relationship. For example, in one dream, Kim dreamt that I was doing something that had no basis in reality but was trying to sow a seed of doubt about me and moving our relationship forward. On the flipside, Satan can give you what appears to be a warning dream from God when it is not God at all. So be careful about placing too much emphasis on dreams when it comes to discerning who you should marry.

Speaking through others

Satan can also use others to speak through. Generally speaking, a good impression from your family and friends about your prospective partner is a good indicator of a compatible future together. Having said that, this does not mean that just because a person has approval from your family, friends and even pastor or spiritual mentors, that they are the one. I have had this happen on more than one occasion, where men I dated (before Kim) had made good impressions on many people close to me, but they were not the right man for me. In fact, sometimes the enemy can actually speak through others to get you off track. This can be others encouraging you to be with someone or telling you they believe God is in a relationship when it is not of God. It can also work in reverse. For example, only weeks before I was getting married, someone close to me said in essence, "Are you sure you are doing the right thing? Do you think it is of God?" This person meant well and did not have any concerns spiritually about our pairing but was simply making sure we had God's peace. However, at the time the person asked me this, the enemy tried to tempt me with thoughts of fear, "Why is this person saying this? Do they know something I don't about this person? Is Kim really the one? Are we rushing things?" Thankfully, I was able to discern this was the enemy, resist these thoughts and move forward in peace.

Exploiting your desires, weaknesses or insecurities

The enemy has observed you since you were born and knows the areas you are most vulnerable in and how to exploit them. One way Satan can do this is by exploiting your natural desire for the opposite sex. When there is a strong attraction or infatuation when meeting someone, people can be literally intoxicated with love hormones, hindering their ability to apply wisdom. For example, you may be extremely physically attracted to someone who is not a Christian and fail to see the reality that they are a negative influence in your life. Because the hormones you are experiencing are so strong, you rationalise to yourself why you should pursue a relationship with this person and ignore the still small voice of the Holy Spirit and your friends' warnings.

Satan may also exploit weaknesses in your personality. My natural personality tends to be tempted to fear and worry, and Satan used this as a strategy to cause doubt and potentially sabotage my relationship with Kim. Praise God his strategies were to no avail and Jesus had the victory! For others, maybe you are easily tempted to be jealous of others around your potential partner and this is something the enemy tries to exploit. Or maybe you are easily tempted to be lustful or experience shame or condemnation from your past. It's important to be alert and once you are aware of what is happening, resist the enemy and his temptations and as the Word promises- Satan will flee (James 4:7)!

Dwelling on the past

Another way Satan can try to oppose some believers is by getting them to dwell on past relationships. This keeps believers in a wounded state and prevents them from moving forward with the person God has for them. As I mentioned earlier, I was in a relationship where I had a strong emotional attachment that was not God's best for me, which resulted in feeling very broken-hearted when the relationship ended. A couple of months after breaking up, I would still feel emotional and teary thinking about "what could have been". While this person was also initially attempting in many ways to get back together, which did not help the situation (and I quickly realised I needed to cut off communication), Satan was also having a field day in my thinking. What helped heal me from this was receiving God's truth. Rather than listening to Satan's lies in my thinking, "You're never going to meet anyone like this person", "Look at what you walked away from", I would bring to my remembrance all the reasons we were not compatible. I then began to thank and praise God for protecting me from a marriage that I would very likely have been miserable in. The verse which I meditated a lot on that also greatly helped to renew my mind during this time was

Philippians 3:13 *"...but one thing I do: forgetting the things which are behind and stretching forward to the things which are before."* If you are still wounded from a previous relationship, invite the Holy Spirit to help you to let go and "forget" the past which is behind you and instead focus on what is ahead. Then, begin to thank and praise God for the future spouse He has for you.

General opposition

You may also experience general opposition or attacks on you as a couple throughout your relationship as things progress, particularly as you move closer to marriage. This may be attacks on your health, finances, other relationships, work or any area of your life. Satan often does this in an attempt to distract you and get you out of the Spirit and think that God is not with you. For example, within a couple of days of getting engaged, I ended up in the hospital with a bad infection. There were also a number of occasions which Kim did not receive text messages I had sent him, which led to significant miscommunications. Thankfully, we were able to identify this and move forward.

We found in general that whatever opposition we faced, somehow God used it to make our relationship even stronger. For example, despite my hospital stay soon after our engagement, I was able to see a whole new level of how caring and compassionate Kim was by my side at the hospital bed. The miscommunications with the text messages helped us strengthen the way we communicate with each other. Indeed, God promises that He works everything together for the good of those who love Him (Romans 8:28). So even if Satan is trying to hinder your relationship, God can turn things around and make it work in your favour to draw you both closer to Jesus and help your relationship reflect Him more.

It's also important to be aware that not all opposition is the enemy and sometimes a relationship may be difficult simply because the two of you are not compatible or God's best for each other. Applying practical aspects of Chapter 7 will help you discern this.

How to overcome the enemy

We, as born-again believers, have already defeated the enemy through Jesus Christ. Walking this victory out, however, takes diligence. Here are some practical things you can do to walk in victory over the enemy in the area of relationships.

Stay close to God

As detailed in Chapter 1, it is important to prioritise your relationship with God. This will sharpen your defences. If you neglect spending time with God and let your relationship with Him slip, you will be more prone to deception. Also, your time with God mustn't always be just about seeking Him regarding your romantic relationships.

While God wants you to seek His guidance, He also just loves your company and devotion. Making time to enjoy God's Presence and the wonder of who Jesus is by the Holy Spirit, not wanting anything in return helps strengthen our connection to God. As the Word promises, when He is our Hiding Place, we are protected from the enemy (Psalm 32:7).

Stay in the Word of God
The Bible talks about in Ephesians 6:17 having the sword of the Spirit, which is the Word of God, as an offensive weapon against the enemy. Just like Jesus used the Word of God to stand against the enemy's lies (Matthew 4:1-11), we must apply the truth of God's Word in our lives when tempted by the enemy. No matter how busy your life becomes, don't neglect meditating on God's Word and truth.

Praise and thankfulness to God
The enemy hates it when we praise and worship God. It is a mighty weapon against the enemy. Psalm 149:6 says, *"May the high praises of God be in their mouths, and a two-edged sword in their hand"*. Praising God and thanking Him for what He is doing keeps us in the Spirit and more on guard against the enemy's attacks. We are to praise God in any circumstance, whether things are going well or things are not going according to our plan.

Praise is a particularly strong weapon against fear. You cannot praise God and at the same time be worrying or fearful. As I got closer to marrying Kim and I knew very clearly that he was the one for me, my heart was overflowing with praise to God. I had a sense in my heart to celebrate and be joyful regarding our union, and what a celebration our wedding was! This built my faith and strengthened me against any attacks of the enemy as we prepared for our wedding and, more importantly, our marriage.

Practical steps and reflections:
1. Reflecting on past relationships, can you think of any times that Satan may have been trying to deceive or oppose you?
2. What can you do in future to help stay on guard against schemes of the enemy in the area of relationships?

Chapter 9: Waiting with purpose and joy

*For everything there is a season,
and a time for every purpose under heaven
Ecclesiastes 3:1*

When you are waiting to meet the person God has reserved for you in marriage, it can be tempting to feel like you are in some kind of holding pattern or limbo land- that your life is on hold. This is a lie from the enemy! Every day and season we are in is a wonderful and beautiful gift from God that has been handcrafted for a purpose. No matter what season we are in, God has planned in advance good works for a specific purpose that He wants you to fulfil. As it says in God's Word, *"For we are his workmanship, created in Christ Jesus for good works, which God prepared before that we would walk in them."* (Ephesians 2:10).

When you are single, you have the most time, freedom and flexibility available that you will likely ever have, far more when you are married or with a family. Embrace wholeheartedly and with joy the time and flexibility of this season of life to fulfil the good works God has prepared for you! You may think, but I don't know what my calling is. Jesus said the greatest commandment is to love God and love others (Matthew 22:37-29). That is your calling, regardless of your season: to love God and love others. To fulfil this, God will do many good works through you by the enabling power of His Spirit.

Loving God with all your heart
Loving God means taking this season to cultivate your relationship with God and love for Him first and foremost, as detailed in Chapter 1. Loving God means obedience unto Him (John 14:15). Obedience isn't some kind of bondage but a beautiful thing we can do in response to God's love for us and our love for Him. Indeed, there is such joy that can be found in living a life fully surrendered to Jesus and His will and embracing all He has for you. If you want to cultivate your relationship with the Father, Son and Holy Spirit, I encourage you to check out some devotionals I have written during my single years that came from a deep place of intimacy with God. You can download a digital copy for free at www.knowinggod.life.

Love others
The second part of your calling, regardless of the season you are in, is to love others. This may mean helping and encouraging your family, friends, other believers, those who are going through struggles, praying for them, and being a practical assistance to, particularly other single friends or those who do not have a lot of support. We are the body of Christ and when one part of the body suffers, we all do. Serving others also helps us to become more selfless. Selflessness and humility are essential characteristics for when you are married, for marriage is about sacrificially serving one another in love.

Serving God
Your season of singleness is also a great opportunity to serve God in ministry, whether that's at your local church or in other avenues. During my single years, I cultivated different gifts, including writing a number of devotional books, supporting my pastor by proofreading his books, serving at church in the praise and worship team, providing administrative help and teaching at open meetings. Had I got married in my own timeline rather than waiting for God's best, I'm not sure if I would have had the same opportunity to develop these gifts and serve God in this way.

An abundant life
Jesus said that He came to give life and life abundantly (John 10:10). Jesus wants us to live rich and fulfilling lives in fellowship with Him. Don't waste this season of singleness putting off things until you are married. Some people think, "Oh, I'll travel more when I'm married, I'll wait until I'm married to do this or that". James 4:14 says, *"Yet you don't know what your life will be like tomorrow. For what is your life? For you are a vapor that appears for a little time and then vanishes away."* Each day is precious. Go start that hobby, travel to that city, or go on the adventure. Do the things that make you come alive. Not only will it widen your circles and chance of meeting someone, but it also allows you to broaden your appreciation for God's creation and enjoy the life and resources God has given you. Satan wants you to hide away miserably in your home and not live the life Jesus died for

you to have. The Word of God says, *"This is the day that Yahweh has made; let us rejoice and be glad in it."* Psalm 118:24.

I look back on my single years as some of the most fulfilling years of my life. I got to travel the world and see so much of God's creation, including a long-awaited dream of mine- visiting Israel. I also got to invest in and build wonderful friendships, learn new hobbies like restoring furniture, boxing, stand-up paddleboarding, and playing piano, as well as get into the real estate market. I was initially putting off some of these things, including buying a property and travelling to Israel, thinking I would wait until I was married to do this. I felt strongly, however, that God was encouraging me to choose the life I wanted to live now, not in the future, and that is what I did. Of course, you must be led by God in all these things and stay within your realm of grace and resources. My point is God wants you to enjoy the life He's given you- it gives Him glory!

Fulfil the great commission
Jesus said of all believers to *"Go into all the world and preach the Good News to the whole creation"* (Mark 16:15). All of us as believers have been commissioned to go into all the world and share the good news of Jesus. This is to be a cry of our heart, no matter the season we are in. As a single, keep this commission at the forefront of your mind and pray to God for opportunities to share the good news of Jesus in your interactions with others, whether it's your family, friends, acquaintances through work or hobbies, or the person

waiting next to you at the bus stop. As a single, I have seen countless people healed, delivered, commit or recommit their lives to Jesus or grow closer to Him by the Holy Spirit, and it continues now that I am married. Is this a priority in your life? Whenever I've prayed to God for opportunities, He has been faithful in opening doors and conversations to share about Jesus, whether it's a workmate at lunch time, my hairdresser, or a person in the supermarket. The main thing is we are available for Him! I'm still learning, perhaps like yourself, but I do know that the Holy Spirit will lead and guide you as you make room and are available for Him in your daily life. Being available is not being preoccupied with your own cares but having an open heart that is seeking opportunities where you can bring God into the conversation, and then being ready and willing to follow His lead. The more surrendered you are, that is, the more your heart is sold out to wanting to do God's will above all else, the more you will see God move through you by the Holy Spirit to touch those around you.

So in summary - your season of singleness does not mean your life is on hold, it can be a truly exciting and fulfilling and abundant time in your life where you can love God and others, serve Him wholeheartedly and share the good news of Jesus. What is stopping you now from living an abundant life in Jesus as a single? Go out and embrace the beautiful season you are in with joy and purpose!

Practical steps and reflections:
1. Are you currently living an abundant life in Jesus during your season of singleness? If not, why do you think this is the case?
2. Are there any things in your life that you are holding off until you are married that God is saying to do today?
3. How can you be loving and serving God and others during this season?
4. Who in your life can you be praying for and witness to that they may come closer to Jesus?

Invitation

Do you want to be closer to God? Do you want a living and dynamic relationship with Him? God wants this so much! The truth is God loves you so deeply and wants you to come closer in a relationship with Him on this earth and for all eternity in heaven. But one thing separates you from having this relationship- sin. You may think that you are a "good" person but the Word of God declares that we all have sinned and fall short of experiencing the glory of God (Romans 3:23). It also says that because of our sin, we are all deserving of hell (Romans 6:23). The only thing that can cleanse us from our sin and give us a new righteous life free from eternal damnation is the death and resurrection of Jesus.

For the wages of sin is death, but the free gift of God is eternal life in Christ Jesus our Lord
Romans 6:23

Jesus, the Son of God, was perfect and without sin. He came down from heaven as a man and humbled Himself to die for your sins, being crucified on a cross. Three days later, He was raised from the dead, overcoming all the power of sin and darkness. Now, whoever believes in Jesus and turns from their sin unto Him, is forgiven and can enjoy an intimate relationship with God the Father, Son and Holy Spirit, now and for all eternity (John 3:16).

Through the sacrifice He made, Jesus wants to replace your old sinful life with the newness of His by the power of the Holy Spirit. This is what it means to be born-again. You become a new creation born of God and enter God's family. Your old life passes away, and all things become new (2 Corinthians 5:17).

It's not enough to simply believe Jesus exists, go to church or think you're a good person. The only way to come to know God and have a relationship with Him now and enter heaven is to decide to turn away from your sin and surrender your whole life to Jesus.

Jesus is the only way to knowing God- now and for all eternity. If you want to accept God's invitation and receive this new life through what Jesus has done for you, pray the following prayer with all your heart:

Dear Jesus,
I believe You are the Son of God. Thank You for coming to earth to die and rise again for me.
I turn away from all my sin and surrender my life completely to You now. Come into my heart and cleanse me with Your precious blood. I receive Your forgiveness.
Jesus, You are now my Saviour and Lord. I belong to You- my heart is Yours forever, and You are mine. God Almighty, You are my Heavenly Father, and I am Your child. I am now born-again!

Fill me with Your Holy Spirit. Holy Spirit, I give You permission to have Your way in every area of my life. Help me to live every day to please You, God, by the power You provide.
In Jesus name, I pray, Amen.

If you prayed this prayer with all your heart- congratulations! God's Word says that we must confess our faith in Jesus (Romans 10:9). If you prayed this prayer, tell someone (preferably someone who has a relationship with Jesus) about this eternal decision. Find a Spirit-filled local church, get baptised with water and the Holy Spirit (Matthew 3:11, Acts 1:5) and start reading God's Word, the Bible, to learn more about who God is- Father, Son, and Holy Spirit.

The fact that you have become born-again into God's family does not mean that your life will suddenly be without problems. The difference is that now, regardless of what circumstances you face, you can be confident that Jesus loves you and empowers you to live every day in intimate oneness with Him. To help you walk this life, God the Father sent you the greatest gift on earth, the Holy Spirit, to be your personal Helper (John 14:26). Come now and embark on the most incredible journey of all- coming to know God, the Father, Son-Jesus, and Holy Spirit, and sharing their love with the world!

If you have just made this wonderful decision to give your life to Jesus, please email me at the following address: MrsRachelGallagher@outlook.com, so I can personally encourage and pray for you.

"Now this is eternal life: that they know you, the only true God, and Jesus Christ, whom you have sent" John 17:3

Appendix 1: Internet dating tips

Internet or online dating has become increasingly common as a way for Christians to meet a partner. During the seeking phase, you may want to try internet dating, particularly if you don't have many opportunities to meet other Christian singles in your everyday life, which was the case for Kim and me. The tips below are from our experience of internet dating.

Set boundaries
Christian dating apps can be distracting and easily waste a lot of time scrolling through potential matches. It's important to think about how much you want to use the app. For example, you may want to limit it to once a day for fifteen minutes. Setting search parameters within your non-negotiables (e.g., Christian only, within your locality, etc) can also save lots of time and save having to look at people's profiles that you already know would not be compatible.

Be honest in your profile
When setting up your profile, be upfront about your age, height and use recent photos. I have met Christian men who lied about their age on their profile, with one saying they were several years younger than they actually were! Something like age will eventually be revealed if you start anything serious, so why lie about it? It sets a foundation of dishonesty and may turn off a potential match.

The same goes for photos. Rather than use a photo when you were 10 years younger and a totally different body shape, post a flattering photo of your current self. I met many men who looked completely different to their profile photos. You want to meet someone interested in you for who you are now - not how you looked 10 years ago.

Also, be honest in your bio/description of yourself. I made it very clear in my profile that my relationship with God was the most important thing to me and I was seeking a man with the same passion for God and values. While you will still get some contact from people who have different beliefs, you are more likely to attract someone who is like-minded. I also made it clear, as my personal non-negotiable that I felt called to live in the city I was currently residing in. This also helped rule out people who had no desire to live in my location.

Meet in person sooner rather than later
Once you see there may be potential compatibility, try to meet in person sooner rather than later. Online, it is much easier for a person to lie or portray themselves as someone they are not, as they have time to formulate perfect responses. In person, this is much harder to hide. Also, it will allow you to see if there is any personality compatibility or physical attraction early on, which is hard to tell from a photo. People can also deceive you with photos, as

discussed, so seeing them in person can reveal the person for who they are on many levels!

Don't give up too easily

My final point is not to give up too easily. Maybe you have had a bad experience with internet dating, or maybe every time you go on there, it seems like there is no one of potential interest and you are wasting your time. My advice is not to give up too soon just because the right person hasn't come along. If I had given up earlier on internet dating, I would never have met my now-husband. The main thing is that you are being led by the Holy Spirit. If you are adamant that God is not leading you to go on internet dating then you must be obedient. However, if you don't get any specific direction, internet dating can be a useful tool for meeting Christian singles, particularly if you don't have many other opportunities. Keep an open heart and stay close to God to follow His guidance by the Holy Spirit.

Practical steps and reflections:

1. Have you considered internet dating? If not, is this something you should pray about regarding whether it is worth trying?
2. If you are on internet dating, are there any changes you need to make to your profile, search criteria or the way you use it that you think will be helpful.

Appendix 2:
Questions to ask before marriage

Here are some example questions that may be helpful to discuss to determine your compatibility with a potential partner. This is certainly not an exhaustive list but a starting point, some of which were adapted from another published list[1]. There is no particular order for these to be asked, however, as some are of a more personal/sensitive nature, seek God's guidance by the Holy Spirit for the best timing to ask these.

Spiritual questions
- Describe when you were born-again and decided to make Jesus Lord of your life?
- How has your life changed since becoming a Christian?
- How does your relationship with God impact your everyday life?
- What are your thoughts on the role of (1) water baptism and (2) baptism in the Holy Spirit in a believer's life?
- What is your belief about the Sabbath day, and do you practice observing it?
- What do you see as the man's and woman's role in the local church?

- How do you envision our family devotions looking like including who would lead this?
- What church do you see yourself attending if you were to get married?
- How often would we pray and read the Bible together in marriage?
- What are your views on celebrating Christmas and Easter?
- How important is personal witnessing in your walk with God?
- Do you believe that the gifts of the Holy Spirit are for today? What are your spiritual gift(s)?
- Acknowledging we are works in progress being transformed into the image of Jesus, in what one or two areas do you think God wants you to grow the most?

Questions about relationships
- What physical and emotional boundaries do you want to keep before marriage?
- How would you describe your relationship with your parents/siblings? Do you have any unresolved issues with them?
- Can you describe how you handle anger? (e.g., do you raise your voice? Have you ever been violent towards another person or object?)

- Have you been married before? Why did the marriage end, and what have you learnt from the experience?
- When was your last relationship? How did it end? Are you still in contact with your ex-partner(s)?
- Have you had any children before? If so, are they currently part of your life?
- How do you handle conflict in relationships? (e.g., do you avoid confrontation, prefer to talk things through)
- Who are your closest friends?

Lifestyle
- How important are eating healthy and exercise to you?
- Do you have any physical or mental health conditions?
- Do you smoke? What are your views on smoking?
- What are your habits regarding sleeping? Are you an early bird or a night owl?
- How organised do you consider yourself to be?
- Would you describe yourself as neat or messy?
- Do you have any personal habits that might irritate others?

Work and finances
- How would you describe your spending style?

- What are your views on tithing? Do you tithe?
- Do you currently have any debt? Do you plan to in the future?
- What are your current sources of income? Do you lean towards being lazy or a workaholic? How many hours per week do you work?
- Do you travel with your job currently or plan to in the future? If so, how often and where?
- If an employer offered you to relocate, is this something you would consider?

Leisure
- How do you spend your spare time during a typical weekday/weekend?
- Do you currently have any hobbies?
- How much TV/streaming do you typically watch and what types of shows?
- What type of music do you listen to?
- Is there any music/media that you find offensive?
- How much time do you spend using social media per day?
- What are your views on drinking alcohol?
- What would be an ideal holiday for you? Do you have any strong desire for travel in the future? If so, where and when?
- How often do you like spending time with your friends/family in a typical month?

Marriage and family expectations
- Where do you see yourself in the next five years/ 10 years' time?
- What is your view on the role of a wife and a husband?
- What do you think about women working outside the home?
- How do you think housework and cooking should be shared? Who would do what?
- How would you go about making decisions in a marriage? What would you do if we disagree on an important issue in marriage?
- What roles would the husband and wife have when it comes to caring for children?
- What are your beliefs about divorce and remarriage?
- Are there any areas you believe you may need to develop before marriage?
- Do you have any timetable for when you want to get married?
- What are your thoughts about being in a situation where one of us might be alone with someone of the opposite sex? Do you think you should be close friends with someone of the opposite sex when married?
- Do you want to have children? If so, how many and at what age would you want to start a family?

What would you do if we can't conceive naturally? (e.g., would you consider IVF, fostering or adoption?)
- Do you have any strong views about how you will raise a child? (e.g., homeschooling, private school, vaccinations?)

Important history
- Have you been involved in sexual activity in the past? How long ago was this?
- Were you/are you involved with pornography? If so, what did you/are you doing to be free from this?
- Do you currently use or have you used in the past any type of illicit drugs?
- Have you ever been involved in any criminal activity or broken the law?
- Have you ever had periods where you walked away from God? If so, what was the extent and the circumstances.
- Do you currently have any other addictions (e.g., gaming, gambling) or anything else I should know about from your past? (homosexuality, molestation, traumatic event)?

[1] *Some of these questions were adapted from a list compiled by Bethany Beal from Girl Defined ministries available here: https://girldefined.com/136-questions-to-ask-in-a-relationship*

About the Author

Rachel Gallagher (nee Wenke) is a wife, mother and most importantly a follower of Jesus Christ. Pictured with her husband Kim, she lives in sunny Queensland, Australia. Rachel's heart is to help others nurture a deep and close relationship with God the Father, Jesus and Holy  Spirit and experience God's best plan for their life - to bring Him glory and point others to Jesus. Rachel is also the author of a series of devotional books, available for purchase through leading online book retailers or downloaded for free at www.knowinggod.life or via the QR code below.

www.ingramcontent.com/pod-product-compliance
Lightning Source LLC
Chambersburg PA
CBHW052105070526
44584CB00017B/2338